ALISON HUTH

STARTING HORSES WITH
QUENTIN SZERY

WORKBOOK PRESS LLC
187 E Warm Springs Rd,
Suite B285, Las Vegas, NV 89119, USA

Website: https://workbookpress.com/
Hotline: 1-888-818-4856
Email: admin@workbookpress.com

Ordering Information:
Quantity sales. Special discounts are available on quantity purchases by corporations, associations, and others.
For details, contact the publisher at the address above.

Library of Congress Control Number:
ISBN-13:   978-1-957618-36-4 (Paperback Version)
               978-1-957618-37-1 (Digital Version)

REV. DATE: 02/04/2022

Contents

<u>Acknowledgement</u>

Thank you to Cameron Szery and Ben Caslick
for their fine horsemanship photographed for this book.
Geof Huth for his patient support in the production of the text.

About Quentin Szery

Quentin who?

Quentin Szery has been working with horses since he was a small boy growing up in the shadow of the Australian Alps. He can hardly remember a time when he was not in close contact with a horse or many horses. Now in his fifties, his life is still controlled by the equine world. While other things in Quentin's world have come and gone, the horse has always remained.

Quentin presently lives on a property tucked away at the end of a road near the tiny town of Maidenwell. Maidenwell has a pub and a general shop and not much more. It sits in the foothills of the magnificent Bunya Mountains, which are about 250 kilometres almost directly west of Caloundra (Sunshine Coast, Queensland, Australia). The season changes are easily noticeable, although the weather is pleasant and enjoyable most days of the year.

From the end of November until the beginning of February, Quentin resides on this little piece of heaven. Most of the remaining part of the year is spent in various locations across outback Queensland with his mustering crew. Quentin's property is a perfect place to breed and train horses. Horses are started during his months at home and their training is finished on the job mustering.

Note from the Writer, Alison Huth

I call myself the writer because this book and books to follow are a writing job for me and a joint authorship between Quentin Szery and me. He is a very difficult man to keep on task at times, as his wealth of experience, his knowledge, and his dreams of the future often take him off on some random tangent that thoroughly distracts him from the task at hand. My first motivation for writing was simply to collect general information about Quentin and his lifestyle to write a children's reading book. It was to be part of a series of books about interesting people. The aim was to write a nonfiction text that would engage reluctant early readers, especially of the boy variety. (This is still in the boiling pot and partly finished.) However, my first subject, Quentin, is a man with big ideas, big dreams, and a big past. My one little children's book has blown out into a whole series and a matching adult series. For the next two hundred years I think I will be writing this series, sharing a wealth of knowledge and a richness of life related to Quentin Szery the experiences and people that create him (if I don't die of exhaustion first).

My knowledge of riding and training horses is minimal; Quentin's seems inexhaustible, so between the two extremes we have hopefully created a text that can claim the attention of a wide cross-section of the equine-orientated community.

This book is not written as a how-to handbook; it is simply a sharing of Quentin Szery's intimate knowledge and understanding of the horse and how he uses this to effectively start training.

Introduction

Thousands and thousands of years ago, horses were natural, free-roaming creatures, living on the Savannah. This natural environment selected bigger, stronger animals; interactions between horses and humans became common as humans recognised horses' capabilities. A symbiotic relationship between horse and man developed, and the art of modern horsemanship was born.

The horse is an integral part of Australian modern history. As soon as the English arrived on the shores of this land, the horse was essential for transport and the development of our agricultural heritage. As pioneers moved out into the country, the horse went with them. Modern Australia was built on the back of the horse. On every farm there was a horse, and on every outback station there were horses, riders, and horse breakers. Many bushmen, both Caucasian and Indigenous, possessed a phenomenal connection with horses and had the athletic ability and courage to work horses effectively in any terrain and in any conditions. The horse was an essential part of agricultural life and so too were competent and courageous riders.

Australians are renowned for their quality horses and horsemanship. There is some tendency in Australia to downgrade ourselves and think training methods from other parts of the world are superior. History has proved this is just not so. For example, our small country has had Olympic champions in every discipline; our Light Horse Brigade, in World War I, were held in great esteem even by their enemies. Many pivotal battles were won due to the courage and horsemanship of these soldiers. Horses have been, and still are, used extensively for working cattle. We have a huge racing industry and a massive community of people who live and breathe equine competitions and activities. Australian Outback Heritage is synonymous with the horse-riding stockman. Horses are found close to the cities, in rural residential areas, in tiny country towns scattered throughout our mountain regions, and spread across the outback plains. The Australian methods used to start and train horses are well developed and highly effective. The symbiotic relationship between horse and human is an integral part of our history, agricultural heritage, and modern Australian lifestyle.

Quentin's Training Objectives

- Develop maximum potential using a minimum of resistance.

- Build a solid base of trust, security, and understanding between horse and human handler.

- Horse and rider should move in perfect, harmonious motion.

The quest for perfect motion extends beyond the horse to the horseman. The horse and rider should work together in timing and balance. A skilled horseman will be able to smoothly transfer the athletic human movements, such as circling and turning, to riding. The same change of balance, weight distribution, and muscular pressure will be present when riding as they would be when completing these movements unmounted. The moves a rider makes should never get in the way of the horse. A rider who braces the natural shape of the horse and uses his or her athletic ability will have a harmonic balance of motion with his or her mount. Both horse and rider will move together as one unit, neither restricting the other.

(Words written in **bolded italics** are defined in the glossary)

PART 1

Quentin's Core Principles of Horse Training

CHAPTER 1

Quentin's Core Principles

Before beginning to train a horse, it is very important you are clear on why you wish to train the horse and what you aim to achieve by training it. Another important factor is that you are moulding the natural inherent behaviours of the horse. Training does not teach the horse new movement patterns but simply trains the horse to perform these movements on command of the rider.

The following principles are the cornerstone of good horsemanship. Understanding the horse allows the handler to develop successful ongoing strategies and enables necessary adjustments at any point of training. Before starting a horse, it is important that the handler is familiar the basics of horse psychology and knows the purpose of training any particular horse.

The following principles are the basis of Quentin's training methods. At times training methods may be altered and adjusted slightly, however, all alterations are built around these basic principles.

1. Visualise the result. What will your horse be doing?

Will it be a competitive camp draft horse? A trail horse? A competitive show jumper? A horse mustering cattle? A child's pony club horse?

Before beginning any long-term project, it is important that you have a clear picture of where you are heading. The basic starting of a horse is a vitally important foundation for later training. Without this strong foundation, more complex and specific training will prove very challenging.

Be sure of the direction of the training you wish to follow with your horse, and choose a horse that will best fit your purpose. Or choose a purpose that will suit the horse you have.

2. Understand your horse and its natural instincts.

a) Herd instincts

Horses naturally live in herds and therefore have a strong social structure. A group of mares that are closely related live together in the herd and are led by a matriarch who decides on feeding grounds, water holes, and camps. The stallion is usually from an outside herd and only allows young colts to remain. He doesn't lead the herd but is responsible for defending it. He shields the mares and foals from danger and from rival stallions. This strong social structure positions horses to easily accept training.

Horses' acknowledgement of humans as part of their social structure allows us to train horses in a various discipline. Foals that live in a herd respond to training more quickly than those that do not. In a herd, foals are accustomed to responding to stimuli in a controlled manner. The moment a horse acknowledges you, you become a significant part of his or her social life.

Secure social structures create a solid base for handling purposes. Social structure needs to be in place from birth. Foals that are born into a herd are better balanced socially from the start. Interacting with other living creatures is as natural as breathing. Early interaction with foals facilitates the acceptance of humans as part of their social structure rather than a predator or something to be feared.

b) Mare–foal relationship

In a herd, each mare has a unique relationship with its foal. A foal always stands in the shadow of its mother, often within physical contact. If the mare moves away, the foal usually follows. If a foal is racing about testing its legs and danger appears, the mare calls the foal back to its side.

This physical space connection can be utilised when handling a weanling. Stand in the same space that the weanling's mother would stand. Do not stand at arm's length. Close contact is what the weanling is used to, and it feels secure in this space. Once an animal is secure, it is much more likely to learn.

c) Stallion

Stallions have an innate ability to herd livestock because they herd their band of mares and foals away from predators and danger. This is a matter of survival in the wild. This natural instinct can be harnessed so horses can learn the skills of mustering and cattle work. This instinct will allow a handler to train a horse to perform various movements on command.

d) Physical environment

The physical environment has a marked effect on the way a young horse develops. Nutritional needs of brood mares must be adequately met by the physical environment. The physical environment also needs to provide opportunity where foals use their muscles and develop good bone structure.

Sloping country with rocky outcrops and a good natural water point gives mares and foals a healthy environment with plenty of obstacles to negotiate. Generally, young horses that come off this country are easy-moving and more skilled in watching where they are going. Small, closed paddocks without a social structure will not allow this freedom; horses are then at a loss when faced with physical and social challenges they have not previously encountered.

3. Observe and understand a horse's reactivity to stimuli (i.e., flight and fight).

Understanding how a horse will react to a whole series of stimuli is essential to successful training. The handler decides which stimuli will be applied at various times. A stimulus is used in order to create an appropriate response by the horse that will, in turn, lead to a horse becoming a well-trained, working adult horse.

The first stimulus is applied when the foal is very young. Being in close proximity to the foal and touching it will create a calm response to humans, which will later make the horse easier to handle.

As the handler works directly with the horse,

which commences around nine to twelve months, more and more stimuli will be provided in order to elicit an appropriate response. The starting process is concluded around three years of age, but training continues for the lifetime of the horse.

When the weanling is removed from its mother at nine to twelve months, it is likely to be insecure, and the handler offers it security dominated by the handler's presence. The handler takes the place of the mare in the weanling's life. The stimulus is the removal of the weanling from its mother, and the desired response is the weanling accepting the handler as its de facto mother.

From this position, the handler starts providing it with food, new experiences, and new environments, gradually increasing its familiarity and acceptance of the handler as a dominant herd member. Through this stage, the horse is handled in many ways, such as worming and veterinary services.

1. Teach on a need-to-know basis.

After the stage of bonding with the weanling, it is essential that the handler is clear on the final desired result of training. Initially, choose the breed of horse that suits the intended purpose. If not familiar with breeds and their capabilities, ask an experienced horseman. Choosing the right breed of horse is essential for effective training.

For what specific purpose is the horse being trained? Identify what skills are required in order to fulfil the intended purpose and concentrate on those skills. Keep training focused and specific, simple, and uncomplicated. Teach on a need-to-know basis. For example, horses that are going to be used in the cattle industry need to be exposed to cattle, not to show jumps. If training a horse for the cattle industry, the stimulus the handler provides would mirror the movements required to work with cattle in any situation. With experience and exposure, horses will excel in this particular field. A horse that is going to be used to work with cattle will learn the skills required for this purpose. The horse that is going to be used for dressage and show jumping will learn the skills specific to that discipline.

5. *Pressure and release.*

The principle of pressure/response and release underpins any successful horse training. The pressure provides the stimulus for a response, and when an appropriate response occurs, the pressure is released. Each time the pressure is applied, the horse becomes more familiar with the desired response.

The principle of pressure/response and release involves a series of elements, such as body language, physical pressure, and, at a higher level, actual visual focus. Body language can be as simple as the handler's presence in the yards. An unfamiliar horse reacts by moving away. This action can be purposeful, instigating a reaction.

A physical pressure is when a force is applied to the body of a horse so the horse will physically respond to that pressure. For example, leg pressure will instigate movement of the horse's body. When riding, visual focus has a direct effect on a trained horse. When a rider visually focuses on something, this is automatically transmitted to the horse via the hands, the balance of weight, the seat, and the legs. The trained horse can feel the focus of the rider. The pressure in this instance is the rider's body movement and weight distribution, and the release occurs when the horse responds.

6. Understand the tools and equipment.

The basic tools used to develop pressure/response and release have been used since the beginning of modern horsemanship. Equipment, such as saddles, bridles, bits, spurs, and head gear, has been refined to suit the purposes of specific equine discipline. For example, the saddle used to perform cattle work is completely different from the saddle used to compete in dressage. Even a horse's type of shoes differs from discipline to discipline.

The equipment itself is not as important as how it is used. Any piece of equipment, if used correctly, can enhance the training process.

7. Imagine how the horse would view the world of training.

The overriding factor about how to treat a horse during training should be based on how the handler would respond in the same situation. For example, a person learning a new skill is usually in a state of heightened focus and slight anxiety. If the instructions given are unclear or inconsistent, this will increase anxiety and decrease the learner's ability to comfortably and effectively learn the new skill.

The response of the horse to training is directly dependent on its perception of what the handler is doing. The handler needs to be observant and diligent in reading the reactions of the horse. At all times, it is important to keep in mind the expected behavioural reactions to any interaction between human and horse. The aim is to develop and refine a strong *symbiotic relationship* between horse and human. A positive psychological link needs to be created. When training a horse, always ask, "Would I like to be treated in the manner in which I am treating the horse?"

PART 2

Quentin's Process of Training

The overriding principle at every stage is the pressure/response and release process. At each stage, ensure the horse is familiar and comfortable with the request for a particular response and is confident, calm, and consistent in giving that response. If, when you move on to a new stage the horse reacts negatively, go back to the previous stage until the horse is confident and calm again. Ensure the horse is fresh and receptive to training. Training needs to be a positive experience for *handler* and horse.

CHAPTER 1

Weaning

- When? Six to ten months of age
- How long? Approximately ten days
- Why now? The foals are easy to handle at this size.
- What? The *weanling* is handled by the trainer and nutrition is maintained by the trainer.

a)   Remove the foal from the mother

Before commencing, ensure the yards are safe with no obstacles, protrusions, or loose wires. Both mare and foal should be yarded apart from the other animals. The mare is then removed from the foal. Lead the mare through the gate. As the foal tries to follow, balk it with your presence until the mare is out of the yard and the gate is secured. The mare is completely and permanently removed from the foal. The mare should be moved as far away from the foal as possible.

b)   **Isolate/draft the foal**

You are now in the position of a surrogate mother. The feeding, watering, and security of the foal have become your responsibility. The foal is now referred to as a weanling. The weanling will now progress through step-by-step training, which will continue throughout its life.

In the first few days following isolation from the mare, the weanling will focus only on looking for its mother. Your presence is required to take up the space. The weanling will gradually associate humans with feeding, watering, and security.

c)   **Catch, approach, and lead**

A symbiotic relationship between human and weanling has developed. The weanling can now be caught. Use a ten-metre hard twist rope with a free-moving loop or ring. Create a loop in the rope by passing the end of the rope through the loop. A rope loop can be thrown over the weanling's head. Alternatively, use a pole or a piece of poly pipe. Cut a notch in the end of the poly pipe and put your loop over this. Hold the end of the poly pipe and slip the loop over the weanling's head.

Throwing a rope over a weanling's head

Allow the weanling to move freely and slowly adjust the rope by gently pulling until it has settled under the weanling's chin and behind the ears.

Slowly apply pressure and release until the weanling is comfortable. As the weanling responds appropriately to the pressure, gradually increase the pressure on the rope until the weanling can be controlled from turning away from you.

Now begin the approach. Every time the weanling tries to move left or right, you should pull it back to face the handler. Step by step, complete the approach to the weanling. If the weanling moves backwards, loosen the rope and allow it to do so. Allow the weanling to stop of its own accord, and then when it has relaxed, start the procedure again. When the weanling is close (approximately one metre away from you), stop and allow it to make the final approach. The weanling will most likely reach out with its muzzle and smell. You should not move but allow the weanling to smell you. If it steps away, no attempt should be made to reach towards it. Instead, you should begin the process again. Once the weanling is comfortable standing close, it should be approached on one side, between the head and the shoulder. Do not touch it on the face. The approach to the side of the neck is a comfortable approach as it is similar to the physical interaction between mare and foal. Touch the weanling on the wither. If it moves away, begin the process again.

The rope is settled under the weanling's chin

Once the weanling responds positively, begin to touch other parts of its body. During this process, continue to softly hold the rope.

When the weanling is relaxed and comfortable within close

proximity to you and responds positively to human touch, the halter can be fitted. Use a rope halter. Feed the long tail around the horse's neck behind the neck rope. Adjust the rope halter up until it is firm. Finish with a bowline.

Applying a britchen to a weanling

Remove the head rope from the weanling. Increase the size of the loop and slip the rope over the hindquarters. This is now referred to as a **britchen**. Keep the weanling facing you and apply pressure to the rope so the weanling moves forward. Walk backwards and gently apply pressure to the britchen so the weanling walks towards your chest. As before, allow the weanling to approach the last few steps by reaching out with its muzzle to smell you. Each time the weanling approaches you, spend time rubbing it up over the head and around the ears. The weanling will become comfortable with being touched and handled in this area. This will position the weanling to accepting the halter and bridle more quickly. It is beneficial to long-term training to spend a substantial amount of time repeating this process until it is second nature to the weanling.

It is vital to remember that the head of the weanling is used to control direction and that movement is initiated from behind. Use the britchen, not the lead rope, to move the horse forward.

d)   **Restrain**

The weanling is now familiar with the lead rope and britchen, responding to pressure applied through them. The weanling can now be tied up. It should be secured to a post, not a rail, and the point of attachment should be higher than the nose of the weanling. Use a **bowline** knot when tying it up.

Weanlings secured to a post

This knot will tighten under pressure but is still able to be easily untied. Ensure knot, lead rope, and halter are in good condition and of a high quality.

The weanling will test the rope and sometimes attempt to

pull back. Leave it to test the rope without human intervention. Eventually the weanling will respond by allowing the rope to remain slack. When it is standing peacefully, the weanling can be released. Repeat this process on a daily basis until the weanling is relaxed and comfortable being tied to a post.

This is a vitally important process. It is essential that the weanling responds comfortably and confidently to being restrained before any more skills can be learnt.

The effectiveness of the weaning process is a vital cornerstone for later training. The steps above should be repeated until the weanling responds in a relaxed, positive way to handling. If at any point the weanling responds negatively, go back to the previous step until it demonstrates comfort and confidence at each step, and then repeat the process.

CHAPTER 2

Second Handling

- When? Two to three years
- How long? Ten to fourteen days
- Why now? The horse is strong and mature enough to handle the physical and psychological challenges of training.
- What? Train the horse to be ridden independently and prepared for further specific training.

a)   Catching

The horse needs to be in a small yard. Enter the yard and wait for the horse to acknowledge you.

Approaching the horse

The horse will demonstrate acknowledgement by approaching and seeking eye contact. Once this happens, move towards the horse by approaching it between the head and the shoulder.

The horse is comfortable being touched on the neck, not the face

The horse finds this approach comfortable as it is a neutral position of interaction. Horses in the paddock will often be seen standing beside one another, shoulder to shoulder, with their hindquarters pointing in opposite directions. They will be simultaneously nibbling each other on the wither.

Stand close to the horse's shoulder. Gently feed the halter under the neck up and around behind the horse's ears. This creates a trap with the nose piece and the halter is tied.

The *halter shank* is tied to a secure post. The point of attachment needs to be above the height of the horse's nose.

b) Mouthing (3–4 days)

Mouthing introduces the horse to the feel of a bit. The horse learns to accept the bit comfortably responding to it and adopting a collected position (break at poll and wither) when being worked. Use a correct-fitting bit, preferably a snaffle or barred bit. Ensure the bars on the bit are wider so the pressure is more evenly distributed. The softer the bit, the softer the horse's mouth will be and the more responsive to the bit.

Placing a bridle over the halter

Do not use chains or leverage as this will lead to a hard mouth and more resistance from the horse. The bridle can be placed over the halter, and then the halter is removed by opening the horse's mouth and slipping the halter down behind the bit. Allow the horse a few days to familiarise itself with the bit. Once it gets used to carrying the bit in its mouth, one rein is passed between the front legs of the horse and attached to the end of a webbing strap. The webbing strap is then placed over the wither of the horse.

Familiarising the horse with the bridle and bit.

Note the horses are in the collected position.

The webbing strap will sit where the saddle would normally sit. The other rein is passed between the front legs and attached to the free end of the webbing on the opposite side.

Ensure the reins are initially not too tight. As the horse becomes more relaxed, tighten them gradually so the horse responds into a collected position. The pressure of the reins and the bit create a response as the horse relaxes in a collected position. Once the horse is in this position, the pressure of the reins and the bit are automatically released. This process can take three to four days minimum and possibly up to a week.

c)   **Long reining (3–4 days)**

This introduces the horse to responding to the particular pressures applied to the bit. It combines the working of the bit with a horse acknowledging the handler.

A *surcingle* is passed around the middle of the horse's girth. The surcingle is placed in the same position on the horse as the saddle girth is usually placed. There is a ring attached to the surcingle on both sides of the horse.

The near side rein is directing the horse,

and the offside rein is being used to tap the horse forward.

The **long reins** are passed through the rings and attached to the bit. The end of the reins should extend well beyond the hindquarters of the horse. (Reins should be around ten metres from the bridle to the end.) Take up a position behind the horse and drive the horse forward lightly, flicking with one rein and controlling the horse laterally with the other rein.

This process begins in a small square yard so the reins can reach the horse from any position. At each corner of the yard, put pressure on the bit to turn the horse towards the centre and acknowledge you. The horse will break at the poll and wither when the bit is pressured and turn laterally towards you. As the horse responds comfortably and consistently, long reining should be done in progressively larger spaces. At the end of this process, the horse should be able to respond comfortably and consistently in large open spaces.

Long reining in a larger space.

Ensure at particular points such as gateways and other changes in physical space that the horse stops and reverses, always breaking at the poll and wither. Collected position should be maintained throughout the process.

The pressure applied in this phase is through the bit; the response is when the horse moves in the direction that you desire. Each time the desired response is achieved, the pressure through the bit is released.

d)   **Leading on horseback (3–4 days)**

Beginning stages of leading.

The control is applied through a lead rope and another more experienced horse called a ***lead-out horse***. The young horse gains security from the lead-out horse, and this extends to acceptance of the restraint applied by the lead rope. The lead-out horse is generally an older gelding that is relatively patient and easy to handle. Leading out a young horse closely simulates riding. The saddle and bridle are introduced to the young horse. A handler is mounted on the lead-out horse and will take the young horse by the lead, holding the lead rope about sixty centimetres from the halter.

Familiarising the young horse with saddle and bridle.

The excess rope will be taken in the hands of the handler and is used to move the young horse along. This is done by gently tapping the horse across the top of the withers with the long end of the lead rope.

Begin leading out in a small yard. The lead-out horse will be beside the young horse. Lead the young horse in clockwise and anticlockwise directions. The young horse will be on the near side one way and on the offside the other way. Initially the young horse should be between the fence and the lead-out horse, minimising the chance of difficulty. Go at a walk and then trot and then canter. Once the young horse is responding well, it can be led on the inside (so the young horse is no longer between the fence and the lead-out horse).

Progress to a large yard and eventually out into the open. This is a very important stage. The more experience the young horse has at this stage, the more settled it will be to ride. Teach the young horse to travel freely beside the lead-out horse. Do circles and stops. Change sides frequently and also teach the young horse to travel in straight lines. This stage should be done over several days.

The young horse will naturally move with the lead-out horse, thus learning to respond to a restriction of the lead rope. The young horse will grow accustomed to the saddle and the rider on the lead-out horse. It will become comfortable and relaxed around a rider.

The pressure is applied by the lead and the lead-out horse, and the horse will respond by moving with the lead-out horse.

CHAPTER 3

Independent Riding

a)   Mounting

At this stage, the horse will become comfortable with a rider mounting it. This will take some patience and perseverance.

Horse is fitted with knee hobbles for mounting stage.

Apply **knee hobbles** to restrain the horse. *It is vital to note that these knee hobbles only remain on the horse in the initial stages of* mounting. *The hobbles should be removed before the trainer sits in the saddle in order to reduce the risk of injury to horse and rider.*

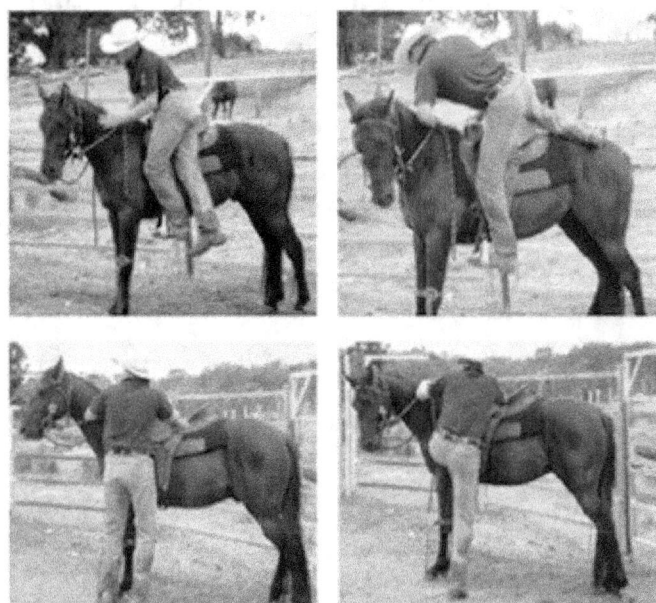

Familiarising horse with mounting.

The rider does not sit in the saddle at this point.

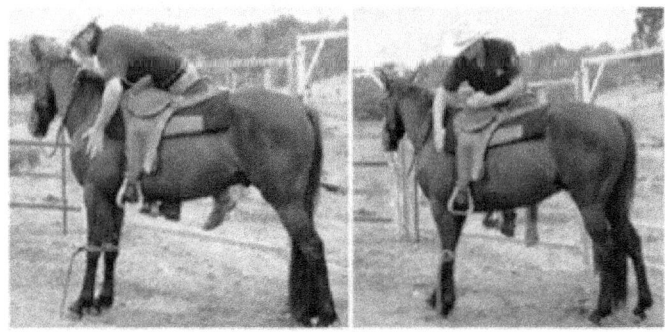

Mount from near side and offside.

Take the bit with the **near side** rein, asking the horse to flex laterally towards you. Weight is placed in the **oxbow** with the left foot. The front of the saddle is held with the right hand and the rein and mane (towards the poll) in the left hand. Gently rise up and down, placing weight on the oxbow, until the horse accepts the procedure. When the horse is comfortable with this action, bend the left knee and run it up the horse's side and over the hindquarter. Continue these two actions until the horse comfortably accepts the initial stage of mounting. Repeat this same process on the **off side.**

Once the horse is comfortable with the initial mounting action, remove the knee hobbles, repeat the same action, and then sit gently in the saddle.

b)   Lead-out riding

The horse is ready to be ridden. *Ensure the knee hobbles are removed.* A halter should be fitted underneath the bridle on the young horse. The young horse is familiar with the lead-out horse and rider. The rider of the lead-out horse places his or her mount across the front of the young horse, taking a **short rein** on the lead-out horse. A lead is attached to the halter of the young horse. Mount using the process of mounting as described previously. Once the young horse comfortably accepts you in the saddle, the rider of the lead-out horse will move his or her horse parallel to the young horse and move forward slowly, taking total control of the young horse by using the lead rope.

Position horse for leading with rider.

As the rider on the young horse, you will do no more than sit, neither requiring a reaction from the young horse nor reacting to the movement of the young horse. All movement is controlled by the rider on the lead-out horse. The purpose of this stage is simply to familiarise the young horse with having a rider on its back. At this point use no crops or spurs.

Make the first ride short, allowing the young horse to feel your weight in the saddle. During this first ride the young horse remains restrained and controlled by the lead-out horse and rider. Trotting and cantering during this ride is acceptable if the young horse is comfortable to do so, but don't coerce this.

Before the second ride, go back through all previous procedures leading up to the riding stage. Begin at long reining and move through leading on horseback and mounting procedures and initial stages of riding. Mount still using the lead-out horse. Trot and canter in the small yard.

c)   Initial independent riding

Final stage of leading out. The rider on the young horse rides passively.

Once the young horse is comfortable with this, move with the lead horse into a larger yard and repeat initial stages with trotting and cantering included. If the young horse responds calmly and comfortably, unclip the lead rope. You and the young horse will now be physically independent of the lead-out horse, but it is important for the lead-out horse to stay in close proximity. The young horse will feel secure next to the lead-out horse, and the lead-out horse and rider will draw the young horse along with their presence.

First independent ride.

The lead horse remains in close proximately.

You will not use the reins excessively at this stage. Gently start taking the bit and allow the horse time to respond. It is important to note at this stage that the young horse may take fright or become insecure at various points.

Begin with walking on the first independent riding.

You need to be nonreactive and calmly settle the young horse if this occurs. Be patient and put yourself in the position of the young horse and how you would respond in a similar situation.

Training simply teaches the horse to perform specific movements on request. The young horse already knows the movements that will be used during riding. It has performed these movements from birth. It learns to read your cues so that it will respond to your directions. Keep cues simple, consistent and clear so that the horse will not become confused and insecure.

d)   Turning

Start to put leg pressure on one side of the horse and then the other. This is so the young horse gets used to the feel of leg pressure. No response by the horse is required. Take the reins and go to one side asking for *lateral flexion*. The young horse will generally *give its nose*, as this has been learnt during the long rein phase. When using the rein to initiate turning, bend your elbow, taking your rein past your body towards the horse's hip, and look in the direction in which you are heading. Allow the horse to break at the poll, and then use pressure with your *outside leg* to complete the turn initiated by the rein pressure.

Asking for lateral flexion to execute a turn.

Note the position of the rider's head and inside leg.

The combination of leg pressure, arm movement, and looking where you wish to go will automatically cause your weight to go to the outside of the saddle, allowing the young horse to step freely across. (This weight change is an exact replica of the weight change that would occur if you were moving on your own legs and wished to change direction.) Teaching the young horse to turn, should be done step by step and not rushed.

Using weight in saddle to help execute a turn.

The rider's weight is balanced on the outside of the turn.

The rider looks in the direction he wishes the horse to go.

e)   **Stopping**

To teach your horse to stop, it first needs to be moving freely. Ensure the young horse knows how to move freely before attempting to teach it to stop. Begin by moving horse away from the direction in which he wishes to head. A young horse will favour a certain direction, usually either down the fence or across the arena. Turn the horse and go in the opposite direction (for example, if it favours going across the arena, ask it to go down the fence). Ask the horse to move into its non-favoured position and then sit down in the saddle in a ***non-riding position***. Always say 'woo' and then take the rein. With a young horse it is preferable to take one rein as it will break at the poll slightly to that side. As it does this, balance the pressure with the other rein and ease the horse gently down to a stop. Using one rein initially is more effective because if both reins are used equally, the young horse may try to push through the bit pressure and continue to move forward.

f)   Backing

Having taught the horse to stop, it is important not to ride forward immediately. Now teach the horse to back up a few steps from the stopped position. Maintain a collected position, with a minimum of pressure. As the handler, 'think backwards'. Bump gently with your legs slightly forward towards the girth. If the young horse moves forward, restrain with your reins as described above and repeat the process.

Backing up.

One step is enough initially. Once the step has been completed, ride forward. Repeat this process until the young horse responds easily, taking several steps backwards at a time. When the horse is fluent in this skill, take one rein and exert lateral flexion in the backwards move. Step by step, this will teach the horse to reverse in its turn. Use your leg pressure to complete this movement.

g)   Yielding

Yielding the hind and front end is imperative in these early stages. The movement required for yielding is a natural movement of the young horse. Introduce spurs to reinforce the use of leg pressure. Ensure the spurs are not sharp and are used firmly but gently.

Using spurs gently but firmly.

To yield the young horse's hind end, stop and then take the rein (remember, one rein) you initiated the stop with and ask for lateral flexion. Apply gentle but firm pressure with your inside leg.

Yielding the horse's hindquarters.

Usually, a young horse will flex away from your leg and bring its nose towards your boot. Hold the horse in shape with the reins. Increase the leg pressure on the inside, keeping the outside leg off your horse. Use the spur firmly and gently to reinforce this move. This will direct the horse to step its hip across. One step is enough initially. *Keep the front end stationary.*

Yielding the front end.

Once the yielding of the hind end is achieved, request the horse to move its front end.

Stop and take the rein you initiated the stop with, asking for lateral flexion as described previously in hind-end yielding. Put your inside leg slightly forward on the girth and apply pressure, once again reinforcing with the spur. *Keep the hind end stationary.* Think about where you wish the horse to go. Focus on the required movement, and cue the young horse to step across with front feet. One step is enough initially. Feel what your leg pressure and spur are doing.

Yielding the front end.

Once the horse has achieved this, move the horse forward whilst keeping its head in the laterally flexed position. Do this by focusing forward and squeeze with your legs. Now move into a reverse arc.

Performing a reverse arc.

This is when the horse is moving in a circle in the opposite direction to the way its head is pointing. It is achieved by leg pressure alone. This skill is used in a number of equine disciplines.

Side passing is another skill important to many equine disciplines. It is easy to teach once the horse has learnt to yield on cue.

Remember what you are asking the horse to do: feel with your hands, legs, seat, and spurs. Always take your rein past your body and bend your elbow. There should be a straight line from the point from your elbow to your hand to the ring on the bit. Never bring your hand below this point as it will tip your balance forward. In all your turns, your weight should be on the outside of the saddle. You should be able to move your leg pressure from one side to the other. This should establish the lateral flexion of your horse. 'Spare your legs and spoil your horse'. Ask the horse for softness in the mouth and the ribs.

It is important that the young horse learns to move forward easily after completing these work patterns of turning, backing, and yielding. Practise the moves sparingly. Sometimes simply ride forward.

In all handling, ensure the horse is at an optimum level of alertness, energy, and focus to learn effectively. Keep handling sessions simple and short initially. As the horse learns new skills and learns to easily understand the handler's cues, handling sessions may increase slightly in length. Relentless repetition will always wear horses down. Don't dwell too long on any moves, and prioritise correctness. Aim to develop softness in their mouth and ribs. Remember to focus on how you would react in a similar situation. Make work interesting, and once a skill is achieved, move on. The learning sessions should be positive and enjoyable for both handler and horse.

CHAPTER 4

Shoeing and Handling Legs

The last essential progression is for the horse to feel comfortable having its legs and feet handled. The horse will require work on its feet and /or shoeing for the entirety of its life, so it is necessary for the horse to be relaxed.

Because of the previous use of knee hobbles, the horse should accept handling of the front feet. Some horses will easily accept handling of the hind feet also. If there is a negative response to handling its hind feet, the hind leg can be restrained. A simple strap is passed around the horse's neck and settled on its shoulder. The loose end of this strap comes over the top of the wither.

It is then passed around the back of the horse's hindquarter, and the horse is turned towards the handler so it steps over the strap.

<u>Conclusion</u>

Is training finished?

No, it has just begun. The horse is now started for independent riding and is ready for training for a specific purpose (for example, stock work). Each equine discipline has its own procedures for training, and it will take a number of years of careful handling for the horse to reach its full potential in a particular field.

At any stage of training, the horse may need to backtrack in order to reinforce basic independent riding skills. Responding appropriately to the bit is one area likely to need revisiting. If the horse does not respond appropriately to bit pressure, it is vital to return to the long reining phase and ensure the horse maintains the collected position, breaking at the poll and wither during all requested moves.

Horses progress at different rates, and it is important that they can progress comfortably and confidently. Training is a patient process in which the handler and horse work together; it is definitely not a process of forcing human will mercilessly on the horse. A well-trained horse is one that has confidence in the rider and willingly responds appropriately to the rider's requests.

Australian horses and riders have always worked together comfortably as a well-balanced unit. Thorough and purposeful training, when first starting, is essential for later success in working horses effectively. The symbiotic relationship begins at the birth of a foal and continues throughout the lifetime of the horse. Understanding horses, working with them, and tapping into their natural behaviours strengthens this relationship. The positive horse–human relationship has always been an integral part of Australian culture. This culture continues today; horses are important workers, companions, and competitors in our modern world.

<u>Glossary</u>

bowline – A knot commonly used where pressure on the rope tightens it but it is easily undone when pressure is released.

breaking at the poll – Bending behind the head (See horse diagram.)

britchen – Big loop of rope that goes the length of the horse and rests between the hock and tail at the back of the horse (See section on isolate and draft weanling.)

collected position – Collect reins so wither and poll are slightly flexed in the vertical plane.

give its nose – When horse responds to pressure of the rein and flexes laterally.

halter shank – Lead rope

handler – The person who is actively training the horse

knee hobbles – A leather or synthetic strap approximately 1500 mm long and 40 mm wide with a 40mm buckle and two 40mml square rings to allow tail of the strap to feed back through (See photo in mounting section.)

lateral flexion – When the horse will turn its nose at the poll and wither in a lateral (sideways) direction

lead-out horse – An older, trained horse that is used to train a young horse (it leads the way)

long reins – Reins that are attached to a bit and extend approximately ten metres from the bit to the end of the reins. They should extend well beyond the hindquarters of the horse.

near side – Left side of the horse as you sit on it

non-riding position - in the stopping process sit down and relax into the saddle in a neutral position, you do not wish the horse to move in any direction.

offside – Right side of the horse as you sit on it

oxbow – Stirrup

short rein - leading a horse with minimal distance from halter shank to the horse's head

surcingle – A large girth for a horse or other animal

symbiotic relationship – A relationship between horse and human that is advantageous to both

weanling – A foal that has just been weaned from its mother

yielding – To give or respond positively to pressure